HISTORY OF SPORTS

THE HISTORY OF GYMNASTICS

by Brendan Flynn

pogo

Ideas for Parents and Teachers

Pogo Books let children practice reading informational text while introducing them to nonfiction features such as headings, labels, sidebars, maps, and diagrams, as well as a table of contents, glossary, and index.

Carefully leveled text with a strong photo match offers early fluent readers the support they need to succeed.

Before Reading

- "Walk" through the book and point out the various nonfiction features. Ask the student what purpose each feature serves.
- Look at the glossary together. Read and discuss the words.

Read the Book

- Have the child read the book independently.
- Invite him or her to list questions that arise from reading.

After Reading

- Discuss the child's questions. Talk about how he or she might find answers to those questions.
- Prompt the child to think more. Ask: What did you find most surprising about the history of gymnastics? Why?

Pogo Books are published by Jump!
5357 Penn Avenue South
Minneapolis, MN 55419
www.jumplibrary.com

Library of Congress Cataloging-in-Publication Data

Names: Flynn, Brendan, 1968- author.
Title: The history of gymnastics / by Brendan Flynn.
Description: Minneapolis, MN: Jump!, Inc., [2025]
Series: History of sports | Includes index.
Audience: Ages 7-10
Identifiers: LCCN 2024009032 (print)
LCCN 2024009033 (ebook)
ISBN 9798892130806 (hardcover)
ISBN 9798892130813 (paperback)
ISBN 9798892130820 (ebook)
Subjects: LCSH: Gymnastics–History–Juvenile literature.
Classification: LCC GV461.3 .F58 2025 (print)
LCC GV461.3 (ebook)
DDC 796.44–dc23/eng/20240301
LC record available at https://lccn.loc.gov/2024009032
LC ebook record available at https://lccn.loc.gov/2024009033

Editor: Alyssa Sorenson
Designer: Molly Ballanger

Photo Credits: Peyker/Shutterstock, cover (left); Lieutenant Whitman/Library of Congress, cover (center); Everett Collection/Shutterstock, cover (right); Image Source/iStock, 1; Rath/Shutterstock, 3; Alex Bogatyrev/Shutterstock, 4, 5; Salty View/Shutterstock, 6-7; Albert Meyer/The Calne Collection/Popperfoto/Getty, 8; George Rinhart/Corbis/Getty, 9; Sepia Times/Universal Images Group/Getty, 10-11, 12-13; Topical Press Agency/Getty, 11 (left); Luigi Fardella/Shutterstock, 11 (right); JOSE JORDAN/AFP/Getty, 14-15; Suzanne Vlamis/AP Images, 16-17tl; BEN STANSALL/AFP/Getty, 16-17tr; PCN Photography/Alamy, 16-17bl; Dimitri Iundt/Corbis/VCG/Getty, 16-17br; Tim Clayton/Corbis/Getty, 18; Toru Hanai/Getty, 19; Laurence Griffiths/Getty, 20-21; Alex Kravtsov/Shutterstock, 23.

Printed in the United States of America at Corporate Graphics in North Mankato, Minnesota.

This book is dedicated to Nate Potashnick.

TABLE OF CONTENTS

CHAPTER 1

FLIP AND SPIN

A gymnast runs toward the vault. He jumps off the **springboard**. He dives forward.

He pushes off the vault. He is in the air. He flips. He spins. He lands on his feet! Flying through the air is hard. Gymnasts train for years.

There are different types of gymnastics. One is rhythmic. Gymnasts do **routines** to music. They use objects like balls, hoops, and ribbons. Trampoline is another type. A third is artistic.

TAKE A LOOK!

What events do artistic gymnasts do? Take a look!

CHAPTER 2

FLIPPING THROUGH THE YEARS

Gymnastics started about 2,500 years ago! Men in **ancient** Greece **competed**. The first modern **Olympics** was in 1896. Male gymnasts twisted and swung on parallel bars. They showed their strength in events like the vault.

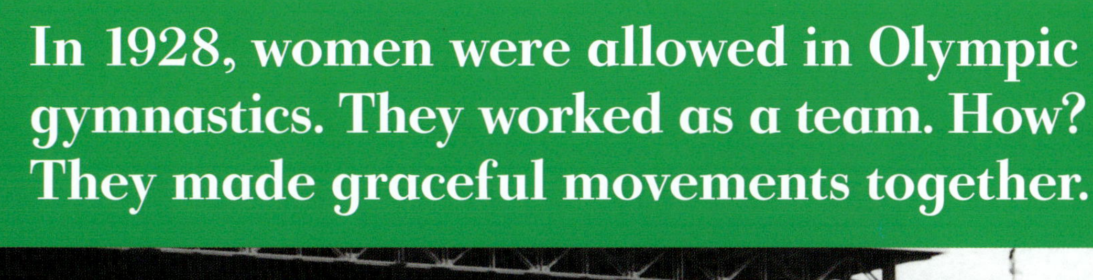

In 1928, women were allowed in Olympic gymnastics. They worked as a team. How? They made graceful movements together.

1928 British women's gymnastics team

In the early 1900s, female gymnasts wore long sleeves. They wore long, loose shorts, too. In the 1930s, they wore shorter and tighter shorts. They wore tank tops. In the 1940s, they started wearing **leotards**. Why? They are easier to move in. At first, they were plain. Now, leotards are bright. Some sparkle. Others have patterns.

TAKE A LOOK!

How have women's uniforms changed? Take a look!

At the first Olympics, men wore pants with belts. They wore long-sleeved shirts. By 1920, they switched to short sleeves or no sleeves. They wore form-fitting pants.

DID YOU KNOW?

Today, men wear shorts for the floor exercise. Why? Pants rub on the mat. They cause **drag**.

The Olympics are an important competition. But there are others. The first World Championships was in 1903. Only four countries were in it. In 2023, people from 80 countries joined!

WHAT DO YOU THINK?

The 1903 World Championships was just for men. Women could not compete until 1934. Was this fair? Why or why not?

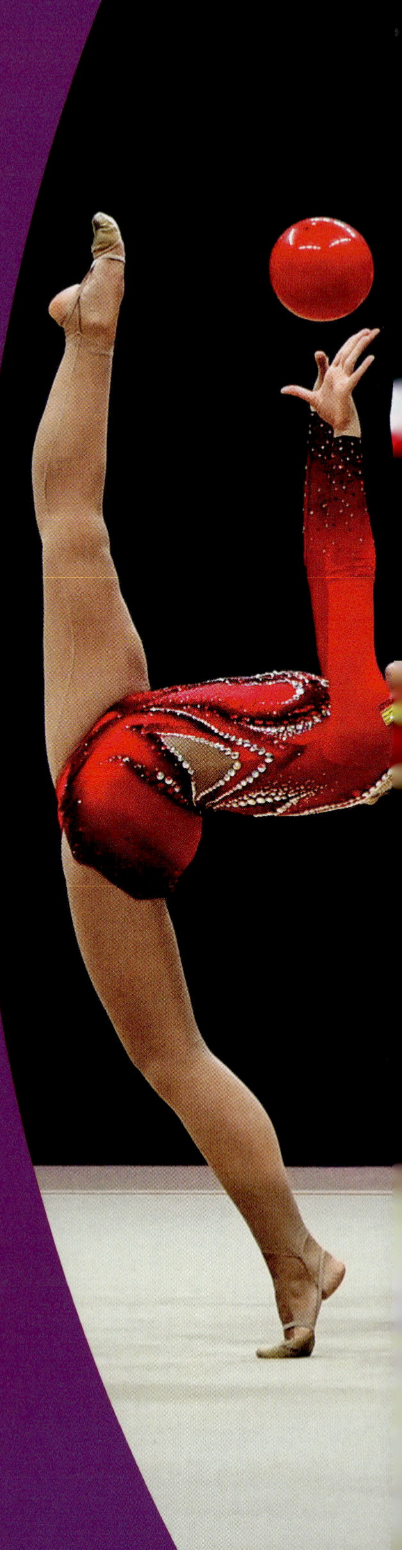

2023 World Championships

Nadia Comăneci

Evgeniya Kanaeva

Gabby Douglas

Vitaly Scherbo

In 1976, Nadia Comăneci went to the Olympics. She was the first woman to get a perfect 10. She won three gold medals. Vitaly Scherbo won six golds at the 1992 Olympics. Evgeniya Kanaeva uses objects like balls, ribbons, and hoops. She won her second gold medal in 2012. Gabby Douglas is a star. Why? She won the **all-around** gold at the 2012 Olympics. She was the first Black gymnast to do this.

WHAT DO YOU THINK?

The top three athletes in an Olympic event win medals. First place gets a gold medal. Second place gets silver. Third place gets bronze. Do you think more than the top three should get medals? Why or why not?

CHAPTER 3

GYMNASTICS TODAY

Once, only men could compete. Now, women are the biggest stars. Suni Lee is one of the best. She was the first Hmong American to win an Olympic medal. When? She won the all-around gold in 2021.

Suni Lee

Kohei Uchimura is from Japan. People call him the best male gymnast ever. He has been to four Olympics. He has won seven medals. Three are gold!

Simone Biles is a **legend**. She is the best gymnast ever. She won four golds at the 2016 Olympics. As of 2023, she had 30 World Championships medals. No one else has that many! She also has five gymnastics moves named after her. Why? She was the first to do them in a competition.

Gymnastics is hard. It takes a lot of practice. Gymnasts are always finding ways to get better!

Simone Biles

QUICK FACTS & TOOLS

TIMELINE

What are the biggest moments in gymnastics history? Take a look!

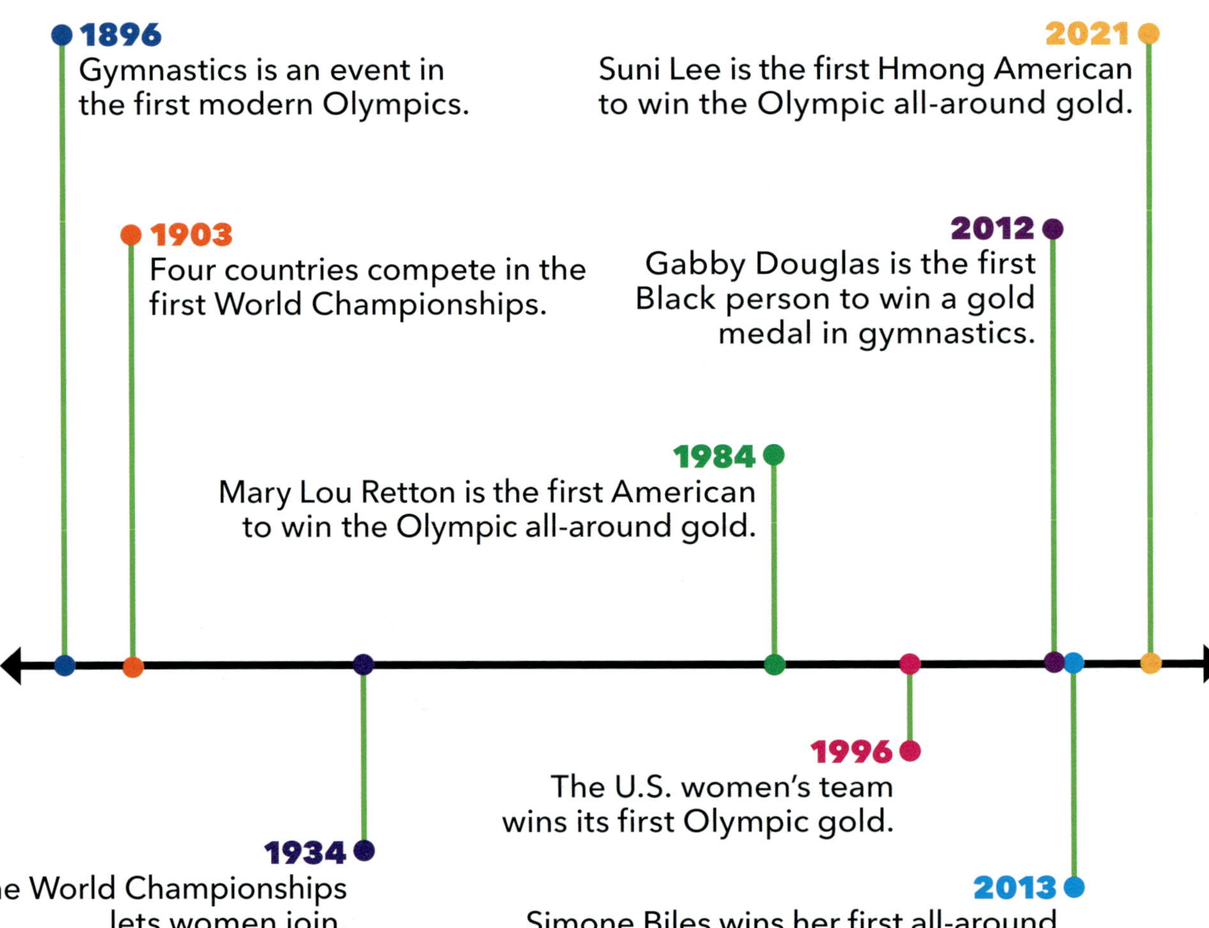

GLOSSARY

all-around: Including all events in a gymnastics competition. The all-around champion is considered the best gymnast in a competition.

ancient: Very old or from the very distant past.

competed: Tried to win a contest.

drag: The action of slowing down motion or advancement.

legend: Someone who is famous or well-known for something.

leotards: Close-fitting one-piece garments worn by female gymnasts.

Olympics: An international competition that features the greatest athletes in many sports. The Olympics are held every four years.

routines: Combinations of moves gymnasts practice and perform.

springboard: A strong, flexible board with springs that a gymnast jumps on in order to get onto a different piece of equipment, such as a vault.

INDEX

TO LEARN MORE

Finding more information is as easy as 1, 2, 3.

1. Go to www.factsurfer.com
2. Enter "thehistoryofgymnastics" into the search box.
3. Choose your book to see a list of websites.